W9-BJB-073

John Dewey

The Founder of American Liberalism

The Library of American Thinkers™

JOHN DEWEY

THE FOUNDER OF AMERICAN LIBERALISM

Amy Sterling Casil

The Rosen Publishing Group, Inc., New York

Published in 2006 by The Rosen Publishing Group, Inc.
29 East 21st Street, New York, NY 10010

Library of Congress Cataloging-in-Publication Data

Casil, Amy Sterling.
John Dewey: the founder of American liberalism/Amy Sterling Casil.
    p. cm.–(The library of American thinkers)
ISBN 1-4042-0508-X (library binding)
1. Dewey, John, 1859–1952. I. Title. II. Series.
B945.D44C37 2005
191–dc22

2005009990

Printed in China

On the cover: A circa 1915 portrait of John Dewey. Background: Hull House circa 1930.

CONTENTS

INTRODUCTION

Education is not preparation for life; education is life itself. *—John Dewey*

The American philosopher and educator John Dewey is often called the founder of American liberalism and progressive thought. Liberalism and progressivism are types of social and political thinking. In almost every way that people can measure human intellectual advancement, our world has progressed since John Dewey's time. Among many of John Dewey's famous quotes is one that is now used for inspiration among athletes and many others: "Arriving at one goal is the starting point to another." This was the way that John Dewey lived his life, and it was the foundation of Dewey's success.

As a young man, John Dewey went to public school in Burlington, Vermont. Dewey's father, Archibald Sprague Dewey, owned a grocery store. Although his family was not rich, Dewey's mother, Lucina Dewey, made sure that all three of her children received college educations. Dewey attended college at the University of Vermont, where he majored in philosophy.

John Dewey was born on October 20, 1859, in Burlington, Vermont. That year, Charles Darwin's famous book *On the Origin of Species* was published. James Buchanan was the president. Around this time, electric lighting was first demonstrated in the United States. And on October 16, 1859, four days before John Dewey was born, John Brown, the famous abolitionist, made his dramatic raid on Harpers Ferry, West Virginia. The trial and execution of John Brown and his fellow abolitionists was a factor in bringing about the American Civil War (1861–1865), which began shortly after Abraham Lincoln was elected president.

In 1859, only white men could vote in the United States. There were an estimated 2.5 million African Americans living as slaves in the American South. In 1830, the year when tensions over slavery began to increase, the estimated value of America's slaves was more than $1 billion. To put this in perspective, the total revenue of the United States' government at that time was only $25 million. It is accurate to say that the majority of men, women, and children in the United States during the year of John Dewey's birth had few, if any, of the rights all Americans share today. Women and people of color did not have the right to attend school, have their own money, own property of any kind, or vote. It was even illegal to teach a slave how to read and write. Some slaves, such as Frederick Douglass, though, taught themselves to read and write, and

In 1859, John Brown led a raid on Harpers Ferry in modern-day West Virginia. Brown was a committed abolitionist who devoted his life to ending the institution of slavery in America. The armory at Harpers Ferry contained tens of thousands of muskets and rifles, which Brown planned on distributing to slaves so they could fight for their freedom. Although Brown's men gained control of the armory, they were eventually captured. John Brown was sentenced and executed on December 2, 1859.

dedicated their lives to educating others about the evils of slavery.

By the time John Dewey was a year and a half old, the American Civil War had broken out. John's father, Archibald Sprague Dewey, had owned several grocery stores before the war. Like many others, Archibald Dewey joined the war effort, selling his stores and entering the Union army as a quarter-master (a person who supplies food and other needed goods). John's family was separated during the Civil War. By the time his father returned, America had changed. The country was united and slavery had been abolished, but President Abraham

Lincoln had been assassinated. More than 620,000 Americans lost their lives in the war, and more than 50,000 others became amputees, losing arms or legs in battle.

John Dewey grew up during this tragic period in American history. This was a time when every aspect of American society and thought was changing. John was strongly influenced not only by his education in philosophy and early psychology, but also by his boyhood experiences in Vermont. His mother, Lucina Rich Dewey, was deeply religious. She taught her son the value of hard work and instilled in him a sense of fairness and caring for others. He wasn't an enthusiastic student in school, but he was a hard worker. He preferred to learn from his direct life experiences.

Traditional philosophy—the ideas of Plato, for example— suggests that there are some fixed or unchanging "truths" that represent reality, and that a person cannot alter these truths. The concept that one person's ideas could change the world beyond himself was thought to be very radical at the time, especially in contrast to traditional philosophical thought. John Dewey's ideas, however, have influenced our lives today in countless ways. Dewey added psychological and logical components to the philosophy of pragmatism. His own teachings were known as instrumentalism, a philosophy that emphasized that a person's memories and education form his or her ideas. According to instrumentalism, a person's ideas can change both the person and the surrounding world.

John Dewey was a doer and a thinker. He believed that people acting together peacefully in a way that he described as "cooperative intelligence" could help create a more equitable, or equal, society. Although he is strongly associated with American socialism, Dewey did not agree with many ideas held by the followers of the socialist philosopher Karl Marx. He rejected fascism and dictatorships, systems of government in which a single person or small group of people control all of society. He also rejected the idea that class struggle was necessary for social change. Instead, he proposed a theory that education and democratic government for all would help create a "cooperative intelligence" for change.

John Dewey also believed that a laissez-faire economy, or one in which the forces of the market controlled everything without any type of government regulation, could not provide a good life for everyone. He said that some people would always suffer, and that a socialized economy, or one that was under government control, would provide everyone with the means for social well-being. The lectures he gave and the books he wrote in the 1930s strongly influenced the New Deal policies of President Franklin Delano Roosevelt. Before the New Deal policies were instituted, retired people did not have Social Security benefits, all young people did not have the right to attend school, and people did not have unemployment benefits if they lost their jobs.

John Dewey wrote a "Pedagogic Creed," or a statement of belief about learning and education. Dewey said that "all

John Dewey lived through the Civil War, which lasted from 1861 to 1865. Eleven Southern states attempted to secede, or break away from, the United States, and form the Confederate States of America. The main reason that the Southern states wanted to secede was that slavery was illegal in the North, and the Southern states, whose economies depended on slavery, were afraid that it also would be made illegal in the South.

education proceeds by the participation of the individual in the social consciousness of the race." Dewey thought that education began at birth, and people engaged in a type of "unconscious education" by their daily participation in society. He also believed in the formal educational system of schools, colleges, and universities, but he had a much broader view of how people could participate more fully in society through lifelong learning and shared social experiences.

Dewey's ideas about learning helped to create the American system of education that exists today. It is hard to imagine a time when teachers taught from a high podium or lectern while a group of select students listened quietly, asking no questions. It is equally hard to imagine a time when school was expected to be hard, boring work all of the time. Dewey introduced the idea of pupil initiative into the classroom. Instead of teachers telling students what to do, students had the opportunity to learn what they wanted to learn, the way they wanted to learn it. As Daniel Schugurensky commented in *History of Education*, John Dewey "brought the teachers out among the students and put the students and teachers together."

John Dewey actively campaigned for women's suffrage, or the right of women to vote. In addition, he fought for the right of workers to have labor unions, for free public education for all students, for world peace, and against child labor. He supported and wrote about Hull House, a revolutionary settlement house in Chicago founded by activist Jane Addams (1860–1935), after which many social action organizations today are modeled. Inspired by another well-known philosopher, Thorstein Veblen (1857–1929), and a group of professors from Columbia University who were fired for opposing World War I (1914–1919), John Dewey founded the New School for Social Research in New York City, where faculty and students together decide what classes are held and what is taught. The New School is still an important educational institution today, and its model has been adopted by many other schools.

When John Dewey died in 1952 at the age of ninety-two, he had written more than forty books and 800 articles that had appeared in more than 150 different journals. Today, more than 4,000 books and articles have been written about John Dewey's life and ideas. The historian Henry Steele Commager wrote in *Thought and Action*, "It is scarcely an exaggeration to say that for a generation no major issue was clarified until Dewey had spoken."

John Dewey's ideas may have been so influential because he always spoke to the public, never directing his writing or speaking to a special, privileged group. Social theorist C. Wright Mills called Dewey in *History of Education* "the last public philosopher, a thinker with a commitment to democracy who always preferred to address the community with issues of public interest than the cold and technical discourse of professional journals and academic lecture halls." A boring day at school may not make students think of John Dewey's revelation that students should be able to have fun learning. But classrooms, teachers, and school activities of today are as advanced as they are because of this man.

John Dewey lived through the American Civil War and two world wars. He was also present for the birth of the American civil rights movement. He was born at a time when many millions of people lived as slaves. For much of Dewey's life, women could not vote or own property, and had little say over their own lives and educations. By the time his long life came to an end in 1952, this had changed dramatically. Some of John Dewey's critics say that not all of these changes were for the better, but very few people today would want to live before these changes were made.

Government programs that help create safe workplaces, organizations that help the disadvantaged, workers who have benefits because of unions, the ability of all citizens to vote, and the thought that people can change the world by changing their beliefs are all legacies of this great American philosopher.

CHAPTER
1

DEWEY'S EDUCATION AND INFLUENCES

Today's teachers believe that one of the most remarkable influences John Dewey has had on education was his understanding of the importance of ordinary, everyday experiences in children's lives. Dewey's own early years in Burlington, Vermont, were like those of many other boys his age. He didn't like school very much, but he did enjoy exploring the outdoors. He lived near Lake Champlain, where he often camped and fished.

John's parents came from different social backgrounds from one another, and his mother, Lucina, was twenty years younger than his father. Lucina was from a

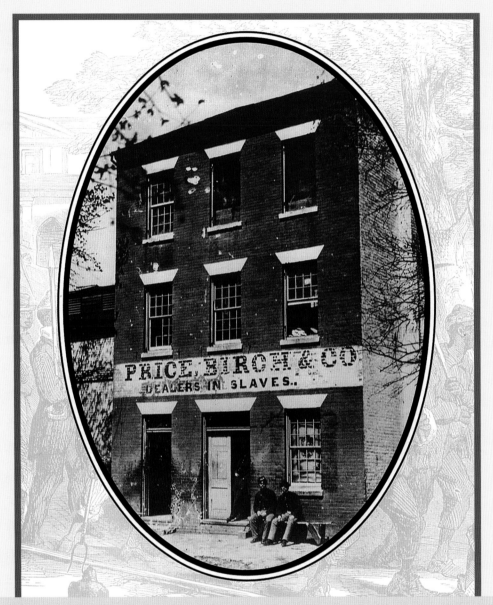

Slavery was a big business in the South, and many profited from this cruel practice. This 1863 photograph shows the Alexandria, Virginia, headquarters of the slave-trading firm Price, Birch & Co. Although importing slaves was banned in the United States in 1808, slave trading within the United States' borders was allowed to continue.

wealthy, well-connected Vermont family. Her grandfather, Charles Rich, had been a member of the U.S. House of Representatives and the Vermont General Assembly. John's father, Archibald Sprague Dewey, was from a family of farmers with a long tradition of working the land.

John's father broke his family tradition by becoming a grocer. He eventually had a chain of stores, which he sold when the Civil War broke out. Archibald Dewey then became a quartermaster for the First Vermont Cavalry Regiment. The family moved briefly to northern Virginia toward the end of the Civil War. When John was ready for school, the family moved back to Vermont. John attended public school in Burlington and graduated from Burlington High School.

At that time, the city of Burlington was becoming known for its rapid industrialization. When John was growing up, farming and agriculture were giving way to factories that streamlined production. Because of industrialization, which meant more jobs in factories, more people crowded into the cities with each passing year. John saw the conflicts between the way of life in the countryside and the way of life in the city.

His later ideas about education and hands-on experiences never represented a desire to go back to the ways of the past. These later ideas were just a simple recognition that most people learn best by doing, whether it is learning to operate machinery, or doing chores on a farm. In his famous book *Democracy and Education*, Dewey wrote, "To 'learn from experience' is to make a backward and forward connection between what we do to things and what we enjoy or suffer from things in consequence."

OFF TO SCHOOL

Schools in the 1860s and 1870s were very different from schools today. Dewey's schools were considered average for their time, but students in New England usually had more complete and thorough educations than students in the rest of the United States. School was seldom fun, and parents and teachers didn't think that it should have been. In his book *Tom Sawyer*, Mark Twain wrote about how kids couldn't wait to get out of school and into real-life adventures (or trouble).

In his book *Our Town: Williston, Vermont*, Richard H. Allen gives the example of a school in the small Vermont town of Williston, which had strict rules that were typical for the time: "That the hours of evening be properly spent by the pupil is deemed to be of special importance. Hence all are required to spend the evening at their homes, or boarding houses, and a proper amount of it in preparation of lessons for the ensuing day. In no case are students allowed to attend parties, or gatherings for amusement, during the term time: nor are they excused from their rooms at all during the evening, except it be by parental authority for the transaction of necessary business, or by special permission of the Principal." It's not hard to see why John would be eager to get out of a school that was so strict, and go fishing, camping, or snowshoeing with his friends instead.

THE UNIVERSITY OF VERMONT

Dewey's mother's family was well educated, and it was taken for granted that Dewey and his two brothers would go to college. When he was only fifteen years old, Dewey graduated from high school and went to the University of Vermont in Burlington. There were only ninety-four students at the university when he enrolled there. Rules for student conduct were strict, but students were encouraged to express their opinions and study anything they wished, including books and ideas that were considered radical, or going beyond the bounds of convention at the time.

In his junior year, Dewey studied geology, biology, and physiology. The textbook in his physiology class was T. H. Huxley's *Lessons in Elementary Physiology*. Although physiology, or the study of the human body and how it moves and functions, was outside of his major in philosophy, Dewey later wrote that reading Huxley's book was an awakening. The way that Huxley showed a connection between human beings and nature inspired Dewey to create a mental model of the way human beings interacted with the world. He formed a theory that he continued to refine throughout his life: science and

Located in Burlington, Vermont, the University of Vermont was established in 1791. Dewey was heavily influenced by the reading he did while attending the school. He was particularly moved by Charles Darwin's *On the Origin of Species*, which detailed Darwin's theory of evolution. The education Dewey received at the University of Vermont would go a long way toward shaping his personal philosophy.

experimentation could be used to solve social and cultural problems.

During his senior year at the University of Vermont, Dewey studied moral philosophy, which included law, history, psychology, ethics, logic, and the philosophy of religion. Moral philosophy was taught by Matthew Buckham, the university's president. Students in the class read John Stuart Mill's book *On Liberty* and William Hazlitt's three-volume translation of

T. H. Huxley and Charles Darwin

Charles Darwin published *On the Origin of Species* in 1859, the same year that John Dewey was born. The book attracted controversy immediately. This famous work, which outlined Darwin's theory of evolution, sold out of its first printing. Its opponents vehemently denied what they believed it said— that people were not created by God, but were instead descended, or evolved, from apes. The book never actually made such a statement, but the revolutionary thoughts Darwin proposed about the natural world and how it changes disturbed those who believed in an unchanging world that was created by God.

Darwin suggested that evolution was a slow, gradual process. But his friend Thomas Henry (T. H.) Huxley believed that evolutionary change could occur in rapid jumps, with species staying the same for long periods of time and then suddenly changing. Scientific research has proven that Huxley was correct. Many evolutionary changes have occurred suddenly. One of the most well-known examples of this phenomenon is the increase in the number and type of mammals following the extinction of dinosaurs many millions of years ago.

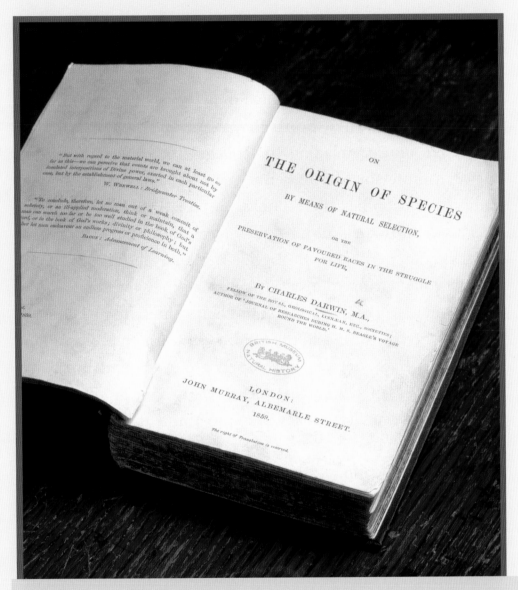

Darwin's seminal work *On the Origin of Species* caused a great deal of controversy at the time of its publication in 1859. Darwin saw no difference between humans and animals, which many people found difficult to accept. Darwin elected not to enter the debate that raged over his theories. Despite the public outcry that continued for many years after the publication of *On the Origin of Species*, Darwin's theories changed science forever.

French historian François Guizot's *Histoire de la civilisation en France, depuis la chute de l'empire romain jusqu'en 1789* (The History of French Civilization From the Fall of the Roman Empire to 1789). These books may not sound very radical, but they were unusual reading for college students at the time. Dewey's professor Matthew Buckham did not believe in the radical philosophies these books proposed. Dewey, however, was inspired by their authors' new ideas and different ways of thinking. In particular, he began thinking about ways that people could change the society in which they lived.

Dewey also studied philosophy with the scholar H. A. P. Torrey, who specialized in the theories of German philosopher Immanuel Kant. Dewey developed a close friendship with Torrey and learned a great deal from him, but he ultimately came to believe that Torrey was too timid in his thinking. Dewey decided that Torrey could recognize conflicts in different systems of philosophy, but he limited himself to describing the conflicts instead of trying to solve them. Dewey began to form his problem-solving approach to philosophy, psychology, and education during his time at the University of Vermont.

Although in later years, John Dewey became interested in many forms of philosophy that were not related to religious traditions, his early life was marked by religious faith. John Dewey grew up in a Congregational Christian household with strong religious values and ideals. During his college years, intellectuals were wrestling with ideas of Darwinian evolution that they were unable to reconcile with traditional religious thought. Dewey later wrote about such conflicts of ideas, calling them "absolutism." He believed that the theory of evolution could be made to agree with religious thought. One of his earliest philosophical goals was to explain religion within a scientific framework. His first two articles, "The Metaphysical Assumptions of Materialism" and "The Pantheism of Spinoza," were published in the *Journal of Speculative Philosophy* in 1882. Both articles sought to bring together specific ideas in religion and science.

GRADUATION

As the end of college approached, it became time for Dewey to choose a career. He considered one in the ministry, a move that his mother, with her strong religious faith, supported. He also considered further education in philosophy. But unlike German schools of philosophy, which were the best in the world at the time, American philosophy departments focused on theology and religious philosophy. Neither of these areas of study appealed to Dewey.

Dewey graduated without a job and spent the next summer looking for work. Finally, an offer for work came through his cousin. He accepted a position teaching at Oil City High School in Pennsylvania. He taught algebra, science, and Latin at the school from 1879 to 1881. It is certain that many

Located in Baltimore, Maryland, Johns Hopkins University has existed since 1876. It was the first college in the country to teach through seminars, in which small groups of students were encouraged to participate in the discussion, instead of teaching classes as lectures, in which an instructor delivers information to a large group of students who are often not encouraged to contribute. Dewey thrived in the environment that Johns Hopkins provided. This circa 1903 photograph shows Johns Hopkins's physical laboratory.

of his influential theories about education were developed in the classroom during his early teaching years.

After writing his first two articles on philosophy, Dewey left Oil City High School and returned to Vermont, where he was the only teacher at Lake View Seminary in Charlotte, a suburb of Burlington. After a few months at the seminary, he applied to study philosophy at Johns Hopkins University in Maryland. Johns Hopkins, which is known today for its hospital as well as its university, was a new university founded in 1876. It was modeled after the great German universities that had separated the study of religion from science and philosophy.

Johns Hopkins

At Johns Hopkins, Dewey met and studied under two fellow Vermonters, philosopher George Sylvester Morris (1840–1889) and the experimental psychologist Granville Stanley Hall (1844–1924). He also worked with another famous philosopher, Charles Sanders Peirce (1839–1914), who is widely credited as being the founder of semiotics, or the study of signs and symbols, in the United States.

Peirce, together with William James (1842–1910), is also considered to be one of the founders of American pragmatism, a philosophy that said that the meaning of an idea lies in its practical consequences. Although pragmatism was still being formed in the 1880s, when Dewey was a graduate student at Johns Hopkins, he became one of the most influential writers in the pragmatic school of thought.

William James wrote a classic series of questions in his 1907 book, *Pragmatism*. James's pragmatic philosophy began by asking about the nature of truth, and whether or not the philosophical truth of a matter was more important than how it affected people's lives: "Grant an idea or belief to be true, what concrete difference will its being true make in anyone's actual life? How will the truth be realized? What experiences will be different from those which would obtain if the belief were false? What, in short, is the truth's cash-value in experiential terms?" It is easy to see how philosophical questions that asked "what concrete difference will this make in anyone's life?" differed from philosophies such as idealism that focus on pure logical argument or ideas that are unaffected by what people might think, say, or do in real life.

Dewey did study idealism at Johns Hopkins, however. Morris introduced Dewey to the theories of German philosopher Georg Wilhelm Friedrich Hegel (1770–1831). Hegel's philosophy of idealism was partially a response to the earlier, also highly influential German philosopher Immanuel Kant (1724–1804). Kant believed that two versions of reality exist: an idealized, permanent, unchanging world of concepts and ideas, and a separate world of daily human experience. Hegel's dialectic, the name that he called the process that combined two seemingly opposing ideas into a unified whole, suggested that people's minds play a role in structuring how they perceive the world, but only in opposition or reaction to things that exist in a permanent, idealized world.

Dewey studied and incorporated the ideas of Kant and Hegel in his own development as a philosopher. Part of his New England upbringing encouraged him to feel that people were isolated from the world and each other, people's souls were

The philosopher Georg Wilhelm Friedrich Hegel, seen lecturing in this illustration, was a German philosopher whose work would have a tremendously wide influence. In the United States, both William James and John Dewey were inspired by Hegel's work. Hegel used dialectics, which Marx would also later use, to explain the history of subjects ranging from art to politics.

isolated from their bodies, and the study of nature was separated from belief in God. This "dualistic" separation was something Dewey sought to bring together for the rest of his life. While he studied Hegel's philosophy, he wrote his doctoral dissertation, the long paper that must be completed in order to receive a Ph.D., entitled "The Psychology of Kant," the philosopher Hegel opposed.

Among William James's many achievements, he is considered one of the fathers of the philosophy of pragmatism. Constantly questioning the world around him, James was deeply interested in religion and psychology. He was also a prolific writer. His book *The Principles of Psychology* is considered a classic, even though some of the material contained within it now seems dated.

THE STUDENT BECOMES THE TEACHER

In 1884, George Morris, Dewey's philosophy teacher at Johns Hopkins, left for the University of Michigan. There he found a position for Dewey as a lecturer, or beginning teacher. During his time teaching at the University of Michigan, Dewey wrote his first important book, *Psychology*, which was published in 1887. He began to combine ideas of idealism and philosophy with new ideas about psychology.

Hegel and Marx

Another philosopher who was influenced by Georg Wilhelm Friedrich Hegel's ideas was Karl Marx (1818–1883). Hegel's dialectic, or theory of opposing forces, was idealistic. He believed that the world was a living thing, which he called *Geist*, or a "living spirit" in German. He believed that world history was like the story of the world's Geist, an ever-developing tale of progress in which people realized certain truths, which became more rational and reasonable as time went on and experience grew. Hegel's idea of progress was not steady and smooth. He believed that a dialectic of opposing views created progress, where one person realizes a partial truth, another person realizes another side of the truth, and

Continued on following page

Continued from previous page

the conflict between the two produces change. In Hegel's view, progress increased wisdom and knowledge.

Karl Marx agreed with most of Hegel's ideas but rejected Hegel's concept that change resulted from spiritual or intellectual ideas. Marx believed that the most important motivating forces in the world were physical and material: food, shelter, money, and goods. His ideas incorporated the dialectic of materialism, not idealism.

Both Hegel and Marx believed that people were in conflict with others and with the world at large because of "alienation," yet each used the term differently. Hegel believed that alienation meant that people's spirits were separated from their physical existence, or that people were alienated from each other because they did not participate enough in their communities. Marx believed that money and greed separated people from each other. His use of the word "alienation" was primarily economic—Marx also believed that the economy created all aspects of society, including art, music, and culture. He thought that a capitalist economic system, in which some people owned factories while others worked in them, created the most alienation of all.

In 1867, Marx published the now-famous first volume of *Das Kapital* (Capital) after observing abuses of factory

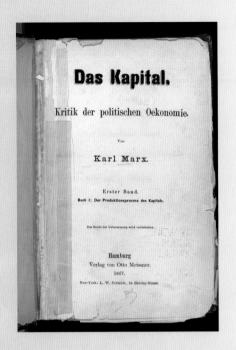

The philosopher and political economist Karl Marx's work *Das Kapital* was an extended critique of capitalism. Although Marx's writings influenced the Socialist and Communist movements that came after him, those principles were usually quite different from Marx's. The first volume of *Das Kapital* was published in 1867. Marx did not live long enough to complete the second and third volumes of the book, which were instead compiled from his notes by Marx's longtime friend and collaborator, Friedrich Engels.

workers in England. The first English edition was published in 1887. Additional volumes were edited and published after Marx's death by his friend and collaborator, Friedrich Engels. *Das Kapital* said that the economic system of capitalism alienated workers from owners and from each other. Marx proposed an economic system to eliminate the abuses of workers he saw, which today is called Marxism. A related system of economics, called socialism, is associated with John Dewey and other American pragmatists.

John Dewey met Alice Chipman while he was a professor at the University of Michigan. Chipman had been a schoolteacher prior to attending the university, and she remained interested in education throughout the rest of her life. Chipman's upbringing had made her acutely aware of social conditions, and many people think that she may have been responsible for pushing Dewey to apply his philosophy to practical matters. This circa 1885 photograph shows Chipman (second from left in the back row) with the Samovar Club, which she and John Dewey had helped found at the university.

Not long after he started teaching at the University of Michigan, Dewey met Alice Chipman, a young student at the university, who moved into his rooming house. In the 1880s, it was common for young people to live in rooming houses while they attended school. Men and women were kept separate, but Dewey probably met Alice while everyone who lived in the house ate dinner, which was a family-style meal prepared by the house's owner. Two years later, Alice graduated from the university and she and Dewey were married. One year later, their first son, Frederick Archibald, was born.

According to author Alan Ryan, Alice Chipman Dewey was one of the most powerful influences in John Dewey's life. Her strong, positive influence motivated Dewey, who was soft-spoken, quiet, and modest, to take a public role in areas where he thought he could benefit society. A remarkable woman in her own right,

Alice was an orphan who was raised by her grandparents in Michigan. Her grandparents were not popular with other white Michigan settlers because they often took the side of the native Chippewa people in disputes over land and property. Alice was taught from an early age to sympathize with and take the side of the poor, minorities, women, and other oppressed people. Alan Ryan writes that Alice's upbringing and strong beliefs gave Dewey three essential ingredients that influenced the rest of his life: fearlessness about ideas and opinions of others, emancipation from organized religion, and a down-to-earth understanding of social justice.

After their mother's death, Alice and her sister Jane wrote, "She had a brilliant mind which cut through sham and pretense to the essence of a situation; a sensitive nature combined with indomitable courage and energy, and a loyalty to the intellectual integrity of the individual which made her spend herself with unusual generosity for all those with whom she came in contact."

Dewey taught at the University of Michigan for ten years, with the exception of one year at the University of Minnesota. During his time at the University of Michigan, he met James Hayden Tufts (1862–1942), another important philosopher and cofounder of the American pragmatist movement. Tufts coauthored *Ethics* with Dewey in 1908. They both left the University of Michigan for the newly founded University of Chicago in 1894. Dewey was hired as the chairman of the university's Department of Psychology, Philosophy, and Pedagogy. At the University of Chicago, Dewey began to lay the groundwork of his most important works in philosophy and education, works that have shaped the world we know today.

CHAPTER 2

DEWEY'S MAJOR ACHIEVEMENTS

Before and during his time at the University of Chicago, Dewey began working to bring together the differences he saw in the various scientific, religious, and philosophical theories that he had studied. He emphasized the idea of "organic unity," or wholeness. He did not believe that the world was made up of the dualisms that he had learned about, such as fact versus value, mind versus body, and individual versus society. He began to believe that society was an organic whole, made up of individual philosophies. In Dewey's new way of thinking, problems in society could be scientifically analyzed.

The Deweys formed the Laboratory School at the University of Chicago, a school for precollege students. In accordance with Dewey's pragmatist beliefs, the school focused on hands-on lessons and student participation. For instance, students would learn about chemical reactions by cooking breakfast together. Despite the grief that Dewey felt at the loss of his son Morris, his time at the University of Chicago was very productive.

Although Dewey's family was growing, he and Alice suffered tragedy when their son Morris, who was born while Dewey was still teaching at the University of Michigan, died of diphtheria on a family trip to Europe in 1894. Diphtheria was a common infection in the 1890s. Today, all babies are vaccinated against it and very few people die of the disease. The Deweys had taken the trip to celebrate Dewey's new job at the University of Chicago. Although his years in Chicago are considered to

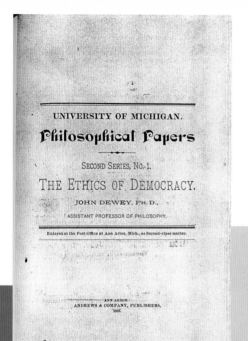

The Ethics of Democracy contained many of Dewey's beliefs about an individual's place in society. Dewey's views on democracy and individualism were groundbreaking for their time. Dewey's beliefs led him to work toward making positive changes in society.

be the most productive time during his long, prolific life, family friends said that Dewey was never the same after Morris died.

In his 1888 book *The Ethics of Democracy*, Dewey argued against the American tradition of individualism. Dewey believed in a social organism that had a life of its own. He thought that people related to each other in a unique way, just as bees lived together in a hive or trees lived in a forest. He highlighted the relationship between paired concepts like product and process, knowledge and knowing, experiments and experimenting, and being and becoming.

Hull House and Social Change

Hull House Association is still an active and vital part of the Chicago community today. Hull House was the original American "settlement house," founded in 1889 by Jane Addams. According to Margaret Luft, former director of one of Hull House's current centers, Addams was one of the first generation of American women who were able to attend college, become highly educated, and form their own opinions about society. They took action to make things better on their own.

Like many other women of her time, including Elizabeth Cady Stanton, who fought for women's right to vote, Jane Addams dedicated her life to community service and social justice. Inspired by a visit to England after she graduated from college, Addams modeled Hull House after a community in London called Toynbee Hall. At Toynbee Hall, she met educated young Londoners who had chosen to live among poor and disadvantaged people. They organized classes, clubs, and recreational activities for everyone in the neighborhood.

What most impressed Addams was that no one looked down upon the less-educated, poorer people in the neighborhood. This was very different from previous charity efforts, which were often characterized by wealthy people giving

Continued on following page

Continued from previous page

material goods to the poor. Sometimes "social workers" were cruel to and judgmental of poor people. This was the last thing that Addams wanted.

In 1889, Addams and her lifelong friend Ellen Gates Starr were given a beautiful house in Chicago by Charles Hull, a retired businessman. Located at the corner of Polk and Halstead streets, Hull's house had once been a country estate. The city had grown around the house, and it was now located in a poor and crowded neighborhood of recent immigrants. Many people called the area a slum.

Addams and Starr opened their doors to their neighbors on September 18, 1889. The situation Addams and Starr faced may sound familiar to people today. Although Hull House opened almost 120 years ago, newspapers were filled with reports about fears of foreigners, anarchists, and unwashed rabble who had no knowledge of American democracy and who were perceived as having no contribution to make to American culture. Many of the problems the immigrants faced were the same as today: extreme poverty, low wages, long working hours, no child care, and lack of health care, education, and safe, decent places to live.

One of the many revolutionary concepts that Jane Addams introduced was the idea that people who wanted to help others should live among the people they were trying to help. Therefore, Addams and all the other workers at Hull House lived there, instead of in a nice, middle-class home somewhere else. She believed in the fundamental dignity of all people, and everyone who came to Hull House was treated with equal respect. She also believed that equal opportunity for education, decent places to live, and a reliable income could change the poverty-stricken lives of the people who lived in the slum around Hull House. Everything that happened at Hull House was designed to achieve these goals and create a better life for everyone in the neighborhood.

Jane Addams's experiment has lasted for more than 100 years, and Hull House programs are conducted through centers around Chicago today. Before Addams's death in 1951, she received the Nobel Peace Prize and many other awards for her pioneering work helping others.

A DYNAMIC ENVIRONMENT

Chicago in the late nineteenth century was a place of rapid growth and change. In many ways, it was not only in the geographic center of America, it reflected the overall societal changes that were taking place. In 1888, the same year that Jane Addams founded Hull House, the United States

Department of Labor was established, marking a key step in the fight for workers' rights.

In 1890, Jacob Riis published his influential book, *How the Other Half Lives*, highlighting the lives of poverty and struggle endured by immigrants in the inner cities. Wyoming became the first state to pass "women's suffrage," giving women the right to vote in state elections. The roots of today's "green" or environmental movement were established when Yosemite National Park was created by an act of Congress, following years of effort by naturalist John Muir and his supporters–the group that would become today's well-known environmental organization, the Sierra Club.

One of the biggest signs of transformation in Chicago was the prominent women and men who had taken leadership jobs in the city, such as Jane Addams of Hull House; Francis W. Parker, a pioneering educator who headed the revolutionary Cook County Normal School; and Ella Flagg Young, the superintendent of the Cook County Schools. She was the first woman to hold such a job in the United States. Impressed by

Born in Illinois in 1860, Jane Addams, as seen in this 1914 photograph, devoted her life to helping others. Hull House, which she founded in 1889, provided disadvantaged people with social and education opportunities. Besides working at Hull House, she also campaigned for world peace. Her dedication to improving social conditions was unflagging, and she lived in Hull House until her death in 1935.

the creativity of these early leaders for social justice, Dewey did all he could to learn about and support their causes. He served on the board of trustees of Hull House and named his third child Jane Mary, who was born in 1900, after Addams. Dewey sent his own children to Ella Flagg Young's new, forward-thinking schools.

Changing the Educational Landscape

In 1895, Dewey wrote a letter to Young explaining the details of a new type of school he had envisioned. He had been hired to be the chairman of the University of Chicago's Department of Psychology, Philosophy, and Pedagogy. Pedagogy refers to teaching techniques and education. Much of Dewey's creative energy in the late 1890s was directed toward developing a curriculum, or series of classes, for the pedagogy department. Dewey argued that the pedagogy department should be separate from philosophy and psychology. Soon, the departments of pedagogy and psychology were separated. By the early 1900s, the pedagogy acquired a name that is more familiar to students aspiring to become teachers today: the Education Department.

In 1896, the University Elementary School at the University of Chicago, also called the Laboratory School, opened. The school put Dewey's revolutionary ideas about education and child development into action. In 1900, the chairman of the

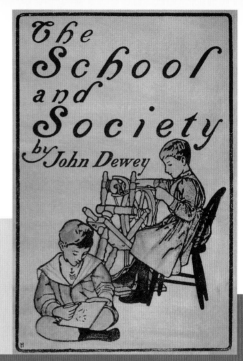

This first edition of John Dewey's *The School and Society* was published in 1899. Dewey's idea that children should learn by doing became a popular one. Dewey believed that, although it was important to teach children facts, it was also important to teach them critical thinking skills.

National Council of Education, Dr. A. B. Hinsdale, wrote, "More eyes are now fixed upon the University Elementary School at Chicago than upon any other elementary school in the country and probably in the world." Parents were eager to send their children to the new school. The curriculum, or areas of study, emphasized the child instead of the subject matter, and the learning process was as important as the subjects that were studied. These ideas may seem like common sense today, but before 1900, they were revolutionary and shocking. John Dewey published *The School and Society* in 1899, which became a classic guide for progressive educators.

Jane Addams's Hull House was the first settlement house in the United States. Settlement houses were local institutions that provided social services to the poor. The philosophy behind settlement houses was that positive social change could come from local communities, and that the greatest progress could be made when communities worked together. The first settlement house was established in England by Samuel Augustus Barnett.

Colonel Francis Parker was also influential in developing the educational curriculum at the University of Chicago. His school merged with Dewey's and eventually, upper grades were added, extending the available education to the high school level. All of the schools were referred to as the Laboratory Schools, and by 1903, the University Elementary School and University High were merged in one building. Students could attend school at the University of Chicago from kindergarten through graduate school, eventually receiving a Ph.D.

Dewey's main educational beliefs, which were shared by Colonel Parker and put into action at the Laboratory Schools, include:

- Learning should be focused on the child rather than the lesson.
- Learning is a social process that is achieved most effectively in small groups.
- Learning should be acquired through hands-on projects, e.g., the study of history through plays, the study of natural science by exploring nature, etc.
- The goal of education should be not only excellence in academics but also creative problem-solving.
- Education should involve developing in students a sense of responsibility to both the school community and larger community.

These children get exercise outside one of John Dewey's Laboratory Schools. Dewey's Laboratory Schools helped him apply many of his educational theories. These theories would go on to influence many other notable thinkers and educators, and change the face of American education.

- The process of learning in a school setting should be a continuation of the type of learning that takes place in everyday life.
- Academic learning should be broad-based and encompass not only traditional subjects but also subjects such as art, sports, music, and various extracurricular activities.

Dewey's "Pedagogic Creed"

John Dewey's theories of child-centered education included hands-on learning. Education connected with democracy in Dewey's mind, and he set forth basic principles about teaching and democracy in several important articles, including an essay called "My Pedagogic Creed," which was published in the *School Journal* in 1897.

Key elements that Dewey considered in "My Pedagogic Creed" include:

Participation: All education results from individuals participating in a social group. Civil societies, in Dewey's view, consist of groups, not "rugged individuals."

Environment: The only true education comes from the stimulation of the child's mind from the demands of the social situation or environment.

Service: The "supreme art" of education should be to give shape to human powers and adapt them to social service. As an example, Dewey suggested that students could help the United States during World War I by working on farms, giving them the idea that serving their country did not have to be destructive to human life.

Experience: Experience brings people together in social participation and renews learning and the life of the community.

Continued on following page

Continued from previous page

Community: Schools, families, political parties, and the general public are all communities. The educational community's job is to overcome over-competitive individualism and encourage group participation.

Activity: Every educational process should begin with doing something, since people learn by doing.

Communication: Words are the ultimate tool by which participation and cooperation occur.

Character: According to Dewey, people can be defined by how they learn. Dewey believed that a love of learning and a desire to serve the community, along with good judgment and human empathy, are key components of a good character.

Higher education: Dewey believed in academic freedom, and in teacher training institutions that would ensure that qualified teachers taught in public schools.

The democratic ideal: The ideal democracy would recognize many different points of view, as well as emphasize decisions based in shared mutual interest.

Democratic culture: Dewey thought that the biggest problem faced by society was the problem of industrialized society relating to human culture. He thought that education was a way to improve culture and democracy.

- Continuing teacher education and research are integral parts of teacher training. Teachers should be given a significant degree of autonomy within a rigorous framework.

John Dewey believed that school could help students to participate in society as adults by helping the students to realize that school already is a version of society.

DEWEY'S PHILOSOPHY ON EDUCATION

Dewey identified two kinds of habits people have that could be adapted in school. The first type of habit is the regular daily routines that everyone follows. Getting up, getting dressed, and getting to school or work on time are all regular daily habits. The second type of habit Dewey identified was that of solving dilemmas, or "creative problem-solving." He sought to create educational activities that would help encourage the ability to solve problems creatively by building a set of experiences that could be applied to many different situations.

Dewey also identified three different kinds of experiences: educative, miseducative, and noneducative. Educative experiences contribute in some way to a student's learning and growth. Miseducative experiences are negative and discourage further learning. Noneducative experiences are neutral—students neither learn nor lose their desire to learn from them. Even a painful experience like burning the tip of your tongue on a hot drink could be educative, in Dewey's point of view. Students would learn to be more careful when drinking hot liquid. Dewey also believed that many traditional school experiences were miseducative. Rote learning, or memorizing facts, drilling, and lengthy tests and recitations tended to discourage students from wanting to learn more. Dewey found that the memory of these tasks was seldom retained by students, and that the activities made them less interested in learning. Categorizing habit and experience in this way enabled Dewey to create a school curriculum and educational philosophy that was revolutionary in its time and which is present in educational training programs and many schools today.

FAMILY MATTERS

In 1904, Dewey's direct involvement with the Laboratory Schools came to an end. His wife, Alice, had been appointed as principal of the school, but her administration was controversial. Disagreements over finances and management caused Dewey to leave the University of Chicago for Columbia University in New York City.

Between schools, the Dewey family took another trip to Europe. In a sad replay of their son Morris's death years earlier, their son Gordon died of the same disease, diphtheria, while

When Dewey was devising the plans for the first of his Laboratory Schools, he didn't want them to have strict rules or teaching methods. Instead, he envisioned the schools as places where experimental approaches to education could be tested. Students were also encouraged to provide feedback on their own learning.

the family was vacationing in Ireland. In 1905, the family adopted Sabino, the first of three children they would adopt over time.

MOVING ON

While Dewey was in Chicago, he had worked in a department of philosophy, psychology, and the new pedagogy, or education

Columbia University, where Dewey began teaching in 1904, is an Ivy League college located in New York City. The move from Chicago was a good one for Dewey, who settled down and worked on refining some of his ideas. The oldest university in New York State, Columbia is considered to be one of the best institutes of higher learning in the country.

department, with people whose ideas were very similar to his. This group of philosophers and educators was known as the Chicago School. Once he was teaching at Columbia University, however, he found himself among a more diverse group, and he began to refine and explain his ideas in more detail. He began to examine his pragmatic philosophical beliefs in more detail, adding a metaphysical component. He also examined his ideals in light of realism and logic, further refining pragmatic thought.

Throughout his long career, the scientific method was always connected to John Dewey's work. After he joined the faculty at Columbia University, he created his mature philosophy and became even more active in politics and social causes. Dewey came to believe that ideas had significant consequences for human life. He thought that ideas could shape the world and place values upon the activities that people conducted every day, from education to politics. He also believed that people could adapt and change depending upon their environment. This idea served as an early basis for behavioral psychology, one of the most important movements in twentieth-century psychology.

Between 1910 and 1922, he published some of his most influential books: *How We Think* (1910), *Democracy and Education* (1916), *Essays in Experimental Logic* (1916), *Creative Intelligence* (1917), *Reconstruction in Philosophy* (1920), and *Human Nature and Conduct* (1922). One of the most important

beliefs that Dewey communicated over these years was the idea that the means and the ends of any activity were the same, especially in a democratic government.

In the Heart of It All

Living in New York City and teaching at Columbia University placed John and Alice Dewey at the center of American political and cultural life. John actively supported the American Progressive Party and served as a contributing editor and frequent writer for the *New Republic* magazine. He wrote so frequently for the *New Republic* that he was paid a salary instead of the usual per-article fee that writers received. He helped to found the American Civil Liberties Union (ACLU), the American Philosophical Society, and the American Association of University Professors (AAUP). In addition, Dewey, along with other prominent Columbia University scholars, founded the New School for Social Research in 1918

John Dewey helped found the American Civil Liberties Union (ACLU), an organization that defends civil rights and civil liberties. The ACLU was formed in 1920 and has been involved in many significant court cases regarding civil liberties. The current president of the ACLU is Nadine Strossen, seen holding a copy of the Declaration of Independence and the U.S. Constitution in this 2004 photograph. In this photo, Strossen is at a press conference for the families of European citizens who are being held without charges in the U.S. prison facility in Guantanamo Bay in Cuba.

in New York City. Dewey and the others did not think they had enough academic freedom and thought that higher education could be improved in the United States. Students and faculty took the leadership at the New School, which was inspired by the London School of Economics and the ideas in Thorstein Veblen's 1918 book *Higher Learning in America*. Veblen soon joined the school's faculty after it opened.

Dewey became a worldwide traveler after World War I, lecturing about education in Japan at Tokyo Imperial University. He spent two years teaching at the Universities of Peking and Nanking in China. In 1924, he studied schools in Turkey, and visited and taught at the University of Mexico two years later. He was asked to visit and inspect the schools in what was the Soviet Union in 1928. When he praised the Soviet schools, many people in the United States criticized him because the Soviet Union had a Communist government and economy, very different from the United States' system of democracy and capitalism.

Dewey believed that a democracy consisted of much more than merely electing people to govern. Dewey knew that democracies could behave "abominably"—for example, the way that America treated minorities in the South. His theory of democracy included the idea that a government should not value the well-being of one citizen over another, and that a government's laws and administration should rank the happiness and interests of all its citizens on the same level.

Dewey always linked his ideas together. He believed that responsible citizens should be well educated, and that education was a key to developing a truly fair and functional democratic government. He also believed that schools should examine the problems shared by all members of society and work to conquer social inequalities. He wanted graduates to be able to consider the needs of society as well as individuals.

Among John Dewey's many profound statements was the observation that he made in *Democracy and Education*, which applies to politics, psychology, and education: "To find out what one is fitted to do and to secure an opportunity to do it is the key to happiness." Even after he retired from Columbia University in 1930, Dewey continued to write, lecture, and be involved in public life. Alice Dewey, who had been suffering from poor health for several years, died in 1927. At age eighty-seven, John remarried, and his second wife was at his side when he died peacefully at home at age ninety-two in 1952.

CHAPTER 3

A LASTING LEGACY

John Dewey was one of the major proponents of the philosophical school of American pragmatism. Unlike many philosophical systems before or afterward, the pragmatists of the late nineteenth century emphasized the role of practical activity in human learning, philosophy, and experience.

Many people have called John Dewey America's Philosopher. For a generation, his ideas about education, philosophy, civic and public affairs, and even human nature and psychology dominated the public discussion. Dewey, along with the pragmatists William James and Charles Sanders Peirce, believed that their philosophy could reconcile the ancient conflict between science and human values. In Dewey's and the other pragmatists' view, human values included aesthetics, politics, and ethics. By emphasizing the role of practical experience in developing philosophies of education and politics, the pragmatists developed a system of thought that helped to bring scientific inquiry and other forms of thought together.

DEWEY'S CONTRIBUTION TO "PHILOSOPHICAL INQUIRY"

While Dewey is referred to as one of the founders of American liberalism and is associated with socialism and other progressive political movements, most scholars refer to pragmatism and Dewey's revision of the philosophy, which was called instrumentalism, as an alternative to Marxist theory and thought. Like Karl Marx, Dewey was inspired by the German philosopher Hegel in many ways, but his interpretation of Hegel's theories was uniquely American.

David Cohen, the John Dewey Collegiate Professor of Education at the University of Michigan, where Dewey spent the early part of his career, wrote in "The Intellectual Legacy of John Dewey" that "no other philosopher in the United States has contributed so much to so many fields of philosophical inquiry." According to Professor Cohen, Dewey was a technically proficient philosopher, but he combined philosophical ideas with the realities of daily life. Dewey's contributions to philosophy were extraordinary because he sought to reorient traditional thinking in almost every way. And, Professor Cohen said, Dewey worked hard to communicate his ideas to the general public, enabling many people to understand them, and most important, put them into practice.

Stanford University professor David Halliburton said in *Essays on Teaching Excellence* that John Dewey's legacy is so "vast and complex" that it is difficult to realize how extensive it is, and scholars must be selective in how they analyze Dewey's work. Dewey placed high importance on communication and its value in teaching and learning. His ideas about communication played a role in the later development of communication theory and the work of behavioral psychologists B. F. Skinner and Carl Rogers.

A Passion for Learning

Professor Halliburton also said that Dewey advocated training teachers like other professionals, including doctors, lawyers, and engineers. He did not differentiate between teaching and learning, considering both to be methods of communication, growth and change. He also believed that when teachers failed, it was because they were unable to get students' "emotional participation." He compared emotions and imagination and wrote about an "emotional intelligence." Today, people take

Psychologist and author B. F. Skinner trains a rat to press a lever in order to be rewarded with food in this 1964 photograph. Skinner advocated a philosophy called behaviorism. He believed that behavior was a result of the positive or negative reinforcement a person received for his of her actions. Skinner thought that behavior could be modified through certain conditioning methods that he developed.

the idea of a passion for learning for granted, but it was a revolutionary idea during John Dewey's early career.

Dewey was as concerned with social equality and justice as he was with education. He wrote in 1935: "No matter how much evidence may be piled up against social institutions as they exist, affection and passionate desire for justice and security are realities in human nature. So are the emotions that arise from living in conditions of inequality, oppression, and insecurity."

Approximately 1,000 Service Employees International Union members gather to voice their demands in Los Angeles, California, in October 2003. Dewey supported labor unions, which have existed for hundreds of years in many different forms. Unions help workers in a given trade organize so that they can demand fair treatment from their bosses.

Dewey's theory of ethics said that the formation of an adequate ethical code would happen only when people based their value systems on human experience in the natural world. Always driven by his ethical concerns and a desire to improve society, John Dewey's vast body of work, written over his long lifetime, led to many changes in our society that people may take for granted today.

DEWEY'S LEGACY OF EDUCATION

The progressive education movement of the 1930s was inspired by Dewey's theories of education, which were first applied at the Laboratory School at the University of Chicago. Student-centered teaching, as well as vocational and hands-on education, were ideas first promoted by Dewey. American public schools today incorporate so many ideas pioneered by the man that it's impossible to say where his educational teaching philosophy stops and modern teaching begins. Teacher training and schools of education at many universities are also part of Dewey's legacy and belief that teachers should have professional education and training not just in the subjects they are going to teach, but in the act of teaching itself.

Dewey also believed that education would help strengthen communities and participation in the democratic process. Far ahead of his time, Dewey was a believer in equal opportunity

These women of the Galena, Kansas, farm labor union pose for a picture in 1936, during the Great Depression. The Great Depression was a difficult time for the United States. One-third of the workforce of the United States was unemployed, stock prices plunged, and the American banking system seemed as though it might collapse. President Franklin Delano Roosevelt instituted his New Deal policies during the Great Depression. FDR was a great supporter of labor unions, and as a result unions made tremendous gains during the Depression.

and access to education. He was also committed to the idea that diversity would strengthen communities, and that everyone should be included in public and community life.

SOCIAL JUSTICE

As a witness to the abuses of the early industrial age, Dewey supported unions and workers' rights. He also strongly opposed the control of many aspects of society and politics by a privileged elite. Improving education, providing equal access and opportunity to learning and jobs, and teaching contemporary events in the classroom were ways that Dewey thought that all people could increase their participation in democracy.

Dewey's commitment to social justice led to his support of organizations like Hull House. Dewey's commitments are reflected in the many charitable and social programs of today, from after-school programs to literacy programs. Dewey believed that without constant vigilance, civil rights could be abused, even in a democracy. His belief in civil liberties led him to become one of the founders of the ACLU, which still promotes civil rights for all Americans today.

The influence of John Dewey's wife Alice increased his focus on social justice. A "freethinker," Alice asked her older children to attend the births of her younger children, so they would gain a more realistic view of childbirth and family

life. Alice's early years in Michigan, when her grandparents championed the rights of the native Chippewa people against opposition from other white settlers, made her strongly committed to the rights of poor, homeless, and otherwise oppressed people. She encouraged her husband's interest in social causes, and together, they made a lasting impact on public policy, which is still felt today.

Programs that were established during President Franklin Roosevelt's New Deal era, which began in the 1930s, are still benefiting people across the United States. In just one example, Social Security provides a reliable income for retired people. Before the establishment of Social Security, many elderly people lived in extreme poverty. Society's assumption was that families would take care of them. Those who lacked families, or whose families were too poor to help, received no assistance. Today, Social Security is also available to disabled people, helping them to live independent, dignified lives.

Franklin Delano Roosevelt is considered by many to be one of the greatest U.S. presidents. He entered office while the United States was at the height of the Depression, and immediately pushed through legislation designed to stabilize the U.S. economy and provide relief for those who were out of work. Roosevelt's programs, known collectively as the New Deal, pumped billions of dollars into public works programs. The New Deal was instrumental to the United States' recovery from the Depression.

This 1934 political cartoon depicts Roosevelt trying remedies on an ailing Uncle Sam while Congress looks on. The bottles of medicine on the end table bear the initials of Roosevelt's social programs. Although his policies generally received praise, not everyone supported Roosevelt's presidency. His opponents thought that his economic plans were irresponsible, and that they actually slowed U.S. recovery.

Some philosophers of the past were concerned with great ideas that were far removed from daily life. Others sought to pursue "perfect ideas," not considering day-to-day practical concerns. John Dewey was not one of those philosophers. David Halliburton, writing in *Change* magazine, said that the most lasting value of Dewey's work can be applied to the social problems that persist in our country: "Now, as then, the hungry and the homeless challenge social resources; crime, drugs, and

This 1935 poster was printed shortly after Roosevelt drafted the Social Security Act. At this time in American history, 50 percent of senior citizens were living below the poverty line, a situation that Roosevelt sought to alleviate. Social Security provided benefits for the elderly and the unemployed.

poverty plague overcrowded cities; and school systems struggle to provide immigrant children with the education they need to survive. In that period and ever since, Dewey, speaking as our most public and intellectual of public intellectuals, has left us a host of ideas on which to reflect."

CHAPTER
4

DEWEY AND PHILOSOPHY TODAY

Following his early study of Hegel's theories of idealism and Kantian ethics, Dewey began making major contributions to American philosophy. His system of instrumentalism modified and added to the pragmatism of Charles Sanders Peirce and William James. Dewey turned away from a system that sought to explain "pure" ideas divorced from day-to-day life and toward his interest in science and the natural world, especially the work of T. H. Huxley and Charles Darwin's theory of evolution. He developed an "empirical metaphysics" that sought to explain ideas using observation of the real world linked to real experiences.

The philosophy of pragmatism is a uniquely American one, and is generally associated with thinkers such as John Dewey, Charles S. Peirce, and William James. Pragmatism was developed at a time when America was undergoing a number of substantial changes and just coming into its own as a country. However, many people believe that the philosophy is still very relevant. Sandra Rosenthal, a professor at Loyola University in New Orleans, Louisiana, is a modern-day proponent of pragmatism.

During his life, John Dewey was one of America's most influential philosophers. He believed that human thought and experience could not be separated from "truth" or "knowledge." His philosophical ideas, however, were criticized during his lifetime, particularly by Bertrand Russell (1872–1970) and other philosophers who were proponents of realism. Though Dewey always communicated with others and worked to clarify his ideas, he believed that most disagreements about his theories were related to the words he used to describe his philosophy. In some cases, he refined, or further explained how he was using different terms, in order to make his ideas as clear as possible. In one example, he defined the word "experience" to mean all aspects of a person's relationship with the environment, not just human thought. Dewey's experience, therefore, included physical, emotional, and spiritual dimensions as well as intellectual thought.

One important but often overlooked aspect of Dewey's philosophy is his ideas about aesthetics, or the study of human expression through creativity and the arts. British philosopher David Hume (1711–1776) discussed the importance of human senses in aesthetics. John Dewey added another dimension to the aesthetic experience, arguing that emotion should be added to pure sensory experience, and that the ingredient of intelligent, reflective emotion created higher levels of artistic expression.

Bertrand Russell was a prolific mathematician and philosopher known, among many things, for his liberal political beliefs. He and Dewey were contemporaries, and when Russell was banned from teaching at the City College of New York, Dewey came to his aid. Along with Horace M. Kallen, Dewey edited *The Bertrand Russell Case*, which was a collection of a number of works discussing aspects of the case.

By the 1930s, the Analytic School in England and other European philosophies, such as phenomenology, became more popular than the work of Dewey and other pragmatists. Like many other fields of study, however, philosophy has become much more open to many different ideas, and the process by which old ideas were discarded and new ideas adopted has become more flexible.

Since the mid-1990s, John Dewey has been revisited by philosophers, and many new critical works have been written about all aspects of his philosophy. He has also been the subject of a number of biographies and other works. Southern Illinois University at Carbondale has sponsored an Internet and real-world project to republish all of John Dewey's writings and to create a complete historical record of his life and work. Many recent philosophers have written about Dewey's ideas and have incorporated them into their work. Writers including Richard Rorty and Jürgen Habermas and philosophers Sandra Rosenthal and James Edie, who are associated with the newer types of philosophy like phenomenology and pragmatism, have written about John Dewey and the other pragmatists.

Many philosophers have influenced many aspects of our lives, from government to education to the way we view the world. According to writer John Shook, as posted on Pragmatism.org, "Dewey ranks with the greatest thinkers of this or any age on the subjects of pedagogy, philosophy of mind, epistemology, logic, philosophy of science, and social and political theory." One of the reasons John Dewey's philosophy remains so influential today is that it is always growing and changing. Jim Garrison, professor at the College of Human Resources and Education at Virginia Tech University, wrote in the *Encyclopedia of the Philosophy of Education*, "Dewey is a philosopher of reconstruction who reconstructed his own thinking several times in the course of his life."

DEWEY'S INFLUENCE

Dewey's interest in education and psychology not only influenced his philosophy, it also had an impact on the field

About Behaviorism

B. F. Skinner

ALFRED A. KNOPF: New York
1974

B. F. Skinner's book *About Behaviorism* was first published in 1974. Written late in Skinner's life, *About Behaviorism* was the basic book explaining Skinner's philosophy of radical behaviorism. Skinner was very interested in Dewey's ideas about behavioral psychology, and used them as a launching pad for his own work.

of psychology itself. Especially influential in the field of behavioral psychology, Dewey's ideas represented a major breakthrough in the study of human behavior. Dewey's article "The Reflex Arc Concept in Psychology," which was published in 1896, is regarded by scholar Thomas M. Alexander in the *Dictionary of Literary Biography* as "his most profound contribution to the science of psychology." The "reflex arc" in the article's title represents previous understandings of human behavior, in that a person who received a stimulus perceived it and then reacted.

Dewey presented a more dynamic, or complex, idea that involved learning and growth. Instead of just waiting for a

stimulus, he described people actively seeking out information and new experiences. According to Dewey, people can create experiences and change the way they act or react based on learning or curiosity about the future. He called these events interactions, and later, transactions. This more complex model eventually developed into the behavioral theories of psychology that we know today.

Psychologists who incorporated John Dewey's ideas into their research and work include Albert Bandura, who developed social-cognitive theory; B. F. Skinner, the premiere behavioral psychologist of the twentieth century; and Carl Rogers, whose ideas about communication closely match those developed by John Dewey more than fifty years before Rogers's ground-breaking work in the 1950s. The ideas that people are part of and interact with their society, that people learn from their experiences, and that ideas and communication can change the world, can all be traced to the early psychological and social writings of Dewey.

Russian scientist Ivan Pavlov was awarded the Nobel Prize in Physiology or Medicine in 1904. Pavlov became famous for his experiments with conditioning dogs. While working on an experiment involving dogs as test subjects, Pavlov noticed that the dogs would begin salivating before their scheduled feeding time. Pavlov realized that this must be an automatic reflex, since they were used to being fed at the same time every day. To test this, Pavlov began ringing a bell whenever he fed the dogs. He discovered that, after a while, the dogs would begin salivating whenever he rang the bell, even if no food was present.

A Lasting Impact

It is John Dewey's ideas about education and democracy that have had the most lasting effect, however. In education, his ideas about a modified child-centered approach to education forever changed the way teachers teach and children learn. His early experimental school at the University of Chicago served as a model that was eventually adopted all across the United States. What was considered radical during the 1880s and 1890s is now standard teaching practice. Dewey's idea that teachers should be trained as professionals is now the foundation of schools of education located at colleges and universities around the world.

Many people are familiar with Montessori schools, the unique system of education founded by Maria Montessori. While not all elements of the Montessori system of education are the same as Dewey's experimental schools, the Montessori focus on children learning by doing was a concept that originated with Dewey. Offering children an opportunity to have a

Famous Italian educator Maria Montessori spends time with young students at a London school that uses her teaching method. The first woman in Italy to become a physician, Montessori founded her teaching method in 1907. Montessori's method emphasized learning by doing, inclusive classes, and an emphasis on student-based learning. Students in Montessori schools learn at their own pace and have control over what they learn.

voice in what, how, and when they want to learn is also an idea that Dewey promoted.

Dewey was not exclusively child-centered, however. He believed that teachers, parents, and students should work together in teams, and that children did not necessarily know everything they needed to learn. Giving them a chance to get excited about learning was better than the curriculum-centered

These Montessori school students use a computer to assist in their learning. Maria Montessori's techniques had a lot in common with John Dewey's philosophy of education. The Montessori method is highly respected, and there are about 4,000 Montessori schools in the United States alone.

approach of teachers who believed they knew best, and the belief that children and parents should have no say in what was taught in classrooms.

Dewey also believed that schools were the ideal place for people of different backgrounds to come together and learn from each other. He recognized very early in his teaching career that education was the key for a strong democracy and a strong society.

BRINGING IDEAS TOGETHER

Because of his early life and upbringing, John Dewey tried to bring the principles of science, particularly his early study of T. H. Huxley and Charles Darwin, together with the ideas of philosophy and ethics. He argued strongly that there were no absolutes and there were no "dualities" of ideas or states of being that could not meet, such as mind and body, or nature and nurture. All things were combined, and the world also changed and grew as people changed and grew.

The thought that people could learn, grow, and change is at the heart of all of John Dewey's work. He believed that society encompassed all of its members, regardless of race, sex, or class, and this led to his commitment to civil rights, democracy, and individual freedom. Not only did he put his ideas on paper, he also put them into practice. His founding of organizations such as the American Civil Liberties Union have helped to defend the freedoms and civil rights of Americans up to the present day. The American civil rights movement of the 1960s, the campaign for women's suffrage, labor unions that protect the rights of workers, and even programs such as affirmative action and equal opportunity laws, all reflect the work and ideas of John Dewey.

CHAPTER
5

DEWEY'S IMPACT

When John Dewey was born, African Americans not only could not vote, they were barred in many states from learning to read and write. Worse yet, many African Americans were forced to live as slaves. Women were not allowed to vote in the United States and had only a few of the rights that all Americans share today. The women of Dewey's generation were the first to attend college and receive educations similar to those received by white men in America. Some of the women with whom Dewey worked while he taught at the University of Chicago were from that generation, including Jane Addams and Ella Flagg Young.

THE KEY TO SUCCESS

Most people today believe that education is the key to success in life. That idea was not clearly stated before Dewey began his work at the University of Chicago and began to write and speak publicly. As Dr. Gordon Ziniewicz, a John Dewey scholar, writes in *Essays on the Philosophy of John Dewey*, "Both Dewey and Plato agree that those who govern should be 'enlightened' or educated." Plato, however, thought that only educated, elite people could properly govern others. Dewey believed in the universal possibilities of education and democracy, and that everyone could be educated and could participate. Dr. Ziniewicz also writes that "faith and optimism are the heart and soul of John Dewey's philosophy." Later philosophies in the twentieth century that were not optimistic originated the idea of pluralism. Pluralism meant that many different people of many different backgrounds coming together could create a pluralistic, or strong, society that comprised diverse parts.

Plato was one of the most influential ancient Greek philosophers. A student of the philosopher Socrates, Plato believed that people should be governed by the educated philosopher-kings. Plato's political philosophy is outlined in his work *The Republic*, which is widely regarded as the most important collection of political science ever written. Plato thought that only elite philosophers who had no other purpose in life than to rule others could be free from corruption.

Dr. Martin Luther King Jr. *(center)*, seen here with other leaders at a civil rights march on Washington, D.C., in 1963, is one of the greatest leaders of the twentieth century. A minister and activist who was a great proponent of democracy and nonviolent protest, King was fundamental in ending segregation in the United States. He was awarded the Nobel Peace Prize in 1964. King was assassinated in 1968, and his work continues to inspire people today.

Today, the idea of diversity reflects William James's concept of pluralism. John Dewey thought about ways that pluralism could work in a practical sense, which led to his theories of education, ethics, and democracy, as well as his refinements and expansion of the basic philosophy of pragmatism. At the end of the nineteenth century, America's economy was changing from an agricultural base to an industrial and manufacturing base. Tens of millions of new immigrants came to the United States during this time. Cities became much larger and far more numerous. In 1860, America had 49 cities with populations larger than 10,000, but by 1900 there were 645 cities that size or larger.

People Coming Together

Much like today, some Americans in the late nineteenth century reacted to this rapid change by calling for a restriction of individual rights, for preventing women and others who could not vote from voting, and for stopping immigration. Dewey did not share this reaction. Instead, he saw the almost limitless possibilities offered by the new immigrants, the potential for everyone to become educated, and above all, the potential that each person had to lead a full, happy, and productive life.

In the *Encyclopedia of the Philosophy of Education*, Jim Garrison described John Dewey as "the man who brought the teachers down among the students." Some have called Dewey "the forgotten philosopher." Seldom has any person been so influential whose name is less known to the average person. Students today do not realize how lucky they are that John Dewey wrote, spoke, and put his ideas about education into action. His egalitarian beliefs resulted in a new and different type of education, which we take for granted today. Students in the nineteenth century could seldom ask questions in class, for example. The main method of teaching was rote learning or memorizing facts, recitation, and oral and written testing. Most teachers never questioned this method of learning, and many students came to hate school and dislike learning. Beyond that, many students were not allowed to attend school, such as the children of slaves, the children of the poor, female children, or children who had to work to support their families.

Liberty, equality, democracy, freedom, equal opportunity, and civil rights are all concepts that John Dewey believed in.

More important, Dewey was able to put his ideas into action. Today's American educational system, methods of teacher training and education, and many other important concepts that are a part of the fabric of our lives, are a direct result of the life and work of Dewey, America's Philosopher and, possibly, our greatest teacher.

TIMELINE

1859 John Dewey is born to Lucina and Archibald Dewey in Burlington, Vermont.

1863 The Dewey family moves to Virginia during the Civil War.

1867 The Deweys move back to Burlington, Vermont. Dewey enters grammar school.

1875 Dewey graduates from Burlington High and enters the University of Vermont.

1879 Dewey graduates from the University of Vermont.

1879 Dewey begins teaching at Oil City High School, Oil City, Pennsylvania.

1882 Dewey publishes his first article, "The Metaphysical Assumptions of Materialism," in *The Journal of Speculative Philosophy*.

1884 Dewey receives a Ph.D. from Johns Hopkins University in Maryland, and accepts a position teaching philosophy at the University of Michigan, in Ann Arbor.

1884 Dewey and Alice Chipman marry.

1884 Dewey publishes *Psychology*.

1886 Dewey publishes *The Ethics of Democracy*.

1886 Dewey accepts a position as chairman of the philosophy department at the University of Minnesota.

1894 Dewey accepts a position in the philosophy department at the University of Chicago.

1894 Dewey's son Morris dies of diphtheria in Milan.

1896 University Laboratory Elementary School opens.

1899 Dewey publishes *The School and Society*.

1899 Dewey serves as president of the American Psychological Association.

1904 Dewey publishes "The Relationship of Theory to Practice in Education."

1904 Dewey resigns from the University of Chicago and accepts an offer to teach at Columbia University.

1904 Dewey's son Gordon dies in Ireland.

1905   Alice and John Dewey adopt a son, Sabino.

1905–1906 Dewey serves as president of the American Philosophical Association.

1908 Dewey publishes *Ethics*.

1909 Dewey publishes *Moral Principles in Education*.

1910 Dewey publishes *How We Think*.

1914 Dewey serves as chairman of the committee that organizes the American Association of University Professors.

1914–1917 Dewey is active in peace movements against World War I.

(continued on following page)

(continued from previous page)

1916 Dewey publishes *Democracy and Education*.

1919 Dewey visits Japan and China, studies Japanese and Chinese education, and teaches at Chinese universities.

1920 Dewey becomes a founding member of the American Civil Liberties Union (ACLU).

1925 Dewey publishes *Experience and Nature*.

1927 Dewey publishes *The Public and Its Problems*.

1927 Alice Chipman Dewey dies after a long illness.

1928 Dewey visits the Soviet Union and studies the Soviet educational system.

1929 Dewey is elected chairman of the National Committee of the League for Independent Political Action (LIPA). He promotes the idea of a third political party.

1930 Dewey resigns as a full professor at Columbia University and becomes an emeritus professor.

1932 Dewey is elected honorary life president of the National Education Association (NEA).

1933 Dewey publishes *Art and Experience* and *Education and the Social Order*.

1934 Dewey publishes *Liberalism and Social Action*.

1935 The John Dewey Society is founded.

1938 Dewey publishes *Logic: The Theory of Inquiry* and *Experience and Education*.

1946 Dewey marries Roberta Lowitz Grant in his apartment in New York City.

1949 Dewey publishes *Knowing and the Known*.

1952 Dewey dies of pneumonia at home in New York. He is cremated, and his ashes are taken to the University of Vermont.

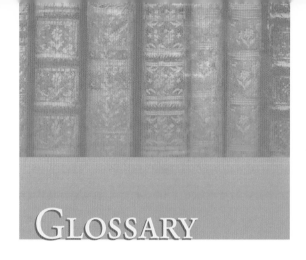

GLOSSARY

aesthetics The study of the philosophy of art, art theory, or art criticism.

capitalism An economic system in which individuals own the production of goods and services, and in which money, investments, and profits or losses are subject to a "free market," or market forces that include supply and demand, instead of the government.

communism A social and economic system that eliminates private property, social class distinctions, and, in its theoretical form, has no "state" or official government.

dialectic Discussion and reasoning by dialogue, using Plato's methods. As described by Georg Wilhelm Friedrich Hegel, it is an idea of the process of change created by two opposing forces.

egalitarianism A belief in human equality, especially with respect to social, political, and economic rights and privileges.

ethics A theory or system of moral values.

freethinker A person who believes that people should form opinions based upon rational thinking that is not influenced by tradition, authority, and established beliefs.

Hull House The settlement house or assistance organization for immigrants founded in Chicago by influential social pioneer Jane Addams.

instrumentalism John Dewey's refinement of pragmatic philosophy. It is a philosophy that says that ideas are instruments of action and that their usefulness determines their truth.

liberalism A political philosophy based on belief in progress, the essential goodness of the human race, and the independence of the individual and standing for the protection of political and civil liberties.

Marxism A political and economic system based upon the ideas of Karl Marx.

metaphysics A division of philosophy that is concerned with the fundamental nature of reality and being.

New Deal The series of acts, government programs, and departments established by U.S. president Franklin D. Roosevelt in response to the economic downturn of the Great Depression and to other social problems.

pedagogy The study of and theories related to systems of teaching and methods of learning.

pragmatism An American movement in philosophy founded by C. S. Peirce and William James that is marked by doctrines saying that the meaning of conceptions is to be sought in their practical bearings, that the function of thought is to guide action, and that truth is to be tested by the practical consequences of belief.

progressivism A political and social movement believing in moderate political change and social improvement by governmental action.

realism A philosophical belief accepting that objects, people, or ideas exist independently of individual experiences, beliefs, or philosophical theories.

scientific method The process by which scientists, collectively and over time, try to construct an accurate, reliable and consistent representation of the world.

socialism Economic and political theories advocating collective or governmental ownership and administration of the means of production and distribution of goods.

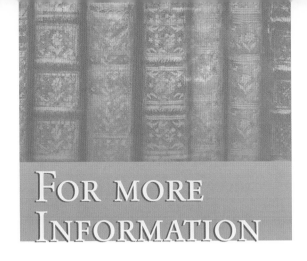

FOR MORE INFORMATION

The Center for Dewey Studies
Southern Illinois University at Carbondale
807 S. Oakland
Carbondale, IL 62901-6822
(618) 453-2629
Web site: http://www.siu.edu/~deweyctr

The John Dewey Project for Progressive Education
University of Vermont
College of Education and Social Services
194 South Prospect Street
Burlington, VT 05401
Web site: http://www.uvm.edu/~dewey

The John Dewey Society
Jeanne Connell (JDS Scty/Treas)
University of Illinois
Educational Policy Studies
375 Education Building, m/c 708
1310 South Sixth Street

Champaign, IL 61820
(217) 333-7328
e-mail: jmconnel@uiuc.edu
Web site: http://www.johndeweysociety.org

The Society for the Advancement of American
    Philosophy (SAAP)
Dr. Kenneth Stikkers
Department of Philosophy
Southern Illinois University: Carbondale Mailcode 4505
Carbondale, IL 62901-4505
(618) 536-6641
Web site: http://www.american-philosophy.org

WEB SITES

Due to the changing nature of Internet links, the Rosen
Publishing Group, Inc., has developed an online list of Web
sites related to the subject of this book. This site is updated
regularly. Please use this link to access the list:

http://www.rosenlinks.com/lat/jode

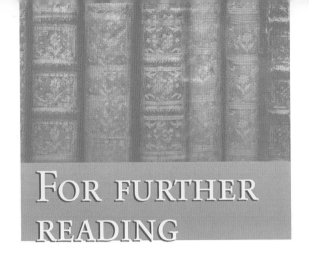

FOR FURTHER READING

Campbell, James. *Understanding John Dewey: Nature and Cooperative Intelligence*. Chicago, IL: Open Court, 1995.

Dykhuizen, George. *The Life and Mind of John Dewey*. Carbondale, IL: Southern Illinois University Press, 1973.

Garrison, Jim, ed. *The New Scholarship on Dewey*. Dordrecht, Netherlands: Kluwer Academic Publishers, 1995.

Hickman, Larry A. *John Dewey's Pragmatic Technology*. Indianapolis, IN: Indiana University Press, 1990.

McDermott, John J., ed. *The Philosophy of John Dewey*. New York, NY: G. P. Putnam's Sons, 1973.

Rockefeller, Steven C. *John Dewey: Religious Faith and Democratic Humanism*. New York, NY: Columbia University Press, 1991.

Ryan, Alan. *John Dewey and the High Tide of American Liberalism*. New York, NY: W. W. Norton & Company, 1995.

Sleeper, Ralph William. *The Necessity of Pragmatism: John Dewey's Conception of Philosophy*. New Haven, CT: Yale University Press, 1986.

Welchman, Jennifer. *Dewey's Ethical Thought*. Ithaca, NY: Cornell University Press, 1995.

Westbrook, Robert B. *John Dewey and American Democracy*. Ithaca, NY: Cornell University Press, 1991.

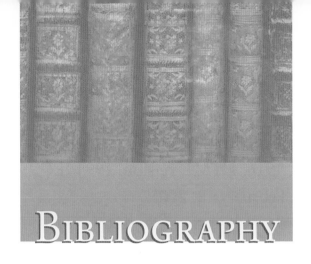

BIBLIOGRAPHY

Alexander, Thomas M. "John Dewey." Dematteis, Philip B., and Leemon B. McHenry, eds. *Dictionary of Literary Biography, Volume 270: American Philosophers Before 1950.* Farmington Hills, MI: Gale Group, 2003.

Allen, Richard H. "Schools in Williston." *Our Town: Williston, Vermont.* Retrieved February 15, 2005 (http://town.williston.vt.us/gen/history.htm).

Anderson, Debra J., and Robert L. Major. "Dewey, Democracy and Citizenship." *The Clearing House,* Nov–Dec 2001, v75 i2, p. 105.

Boyles, Deron R. "John Dewey." Paul Hansom, ed. *Dictionary of Literary Biography, Volume 246: Twentieth-Century American Cultural Theorists.* Farmington Hills, MI: Gale Group, 2001.

Cohen, David K. "The Intellectual Legacy of John Dewey." *Michigan Today.* Summer 1997. Retrieved February 17, 2005 (http://www.umich.edu/~newsinfo/MT/97/Sum97/mta1aj97.html).

Dewey, John. Chapter 11: Experience and Thinking. *Democracy and Education*. Macmillan, 1916. HTML version, 1994 ILT Digital Classics. Retrieved February 12, 2005 (http://www.ilt.columbia.edu/publications/Projects/digitexts/dewey/d_e/chapter11.html).

"Economics at the New School for Social Research." *History of Economic Thought*. Department of Economics, New School of Social Research. Retrieved February 16, 2005 (http://cepa.newschool.edu/het/schools/newsch.htm).

Field, Richard. "John Dewey." James Fieser, Ph.D., Editor. The Internet Encyclopedia of Philosophy. 2001. Retrieved February 16, 2005 (http://www.iep.utm.edu/d/dewey.htm).

Garrison, Jim. "John Dewey." *Encyclopedia of the Philosophy of Education*. October 11, 1999. Retrieved February 16, 2005 (http://www.vusst.hr/ENCYCLOPAEDIA/john_dewey.htm).

Halliburton, David. "John Dewey: A Voice that Still Speaks to Us." *Change*. January/February 1997, pp. 26–29.

Halliburton, David. "The Legacy of John Dewey." Essays on Teaching Excellence. The Professional and Organizational Development Network in Higher Education. Tufts University. Retrieved February 16, 2005 (http://ase.tufts.edu/cae/tufts-secure/v11/v11n8.htm).

"History and Philosophy of the Laboratory Schools." The University of Chicago Laboratory Schools. 2004. Retrieved February 16, 2005 (http://www.ucls.uchicago.edu/academics/ms/handbook/3.shtml).

"John Dewey, Father of Pragmatism." Roots of Early Childhood Education. *Early Childhood Today*. Scholastic, 2005. Retrieved February 16, 2005 (http://teacher. scholastic.com/products/ect/dewey.htm).

Luft, Margaret. Jane Addams Hull House Association. "About Jane Addams Hull House." Retrieved February 15, 2005 (http://www.hullhouse.org/about.asp).

McLellan, David. "Alienation in Hegel and Marx." *Dictionary of the History of Ideas*. The Gale Group. University of Virginia Library E-Text Center. May 3, 2003. Retrieved February 16, 2005 (http://etext.lib.virginia.edu/cgi-local/DHI/dhi.cgi?id=dv1-06).

PBS Online. "Africans in America/Part 4/Map from Coast to Coast." Retrieved February 15, 2005 (http://www.pbs.org/wgbh/aia/part4/map4.html).

"The Philosophy of John Dewey." *The Great Thinkers of Western Philosophy: Classic Philosophers*. The Radical Academy. Retrieved February 15, 2005 (http://radicalacademy.com/phildewey.htm).

Pickens, Donald K. *World Philosophers and Their Works*. Hackensack, NJ: Salem Press, 2000.

Schugurensky, Daniel. "Dewey Advocates Cooperative Intelligence and a Socialized Economy in Liberalism and Social Action." *History of Education: Selected Moments in the 20th Century*. The Ontario Institute for Studies in Education of the University of Chicago. Retrieved February 15, 2005 (http://fcis.oise.utoronto.ca/~daniel_schugurensky/ assignment1/1935dewey.html).

Shook, John. "John Dewey." The Pragmatism Archive, 2004. Retrieved February 16, 2005 (http://dewey.pragmatism.org).

"Thought and Action: John Dewey at the University of Michigan." University of Michigan School of Education. School of Education History. Retrieved February 18, 2005 (http://www.soe.umich.edu/dewey/introduction/).

Walker, Linda Robinson. "John Dewey at Michigan, Part 2. The Birth of Pragmatism, the Philosopher's Second Ann Arbor Period, 1889–1894." *Michigan Today*. Fall 1997. Retrieved February 17, 2005 (http://www.umich.edu/ ~newsinfo/MT/97/Fal97/mt13f97.html).

Waggoner, Ben. "Thomas Henry Huxley." *History of Evolution*. University of California, Berkeley, February 8, 1999. Retrieved February 10, 2005 (http://www.ucmp. berkeley.edu/history/thuxley.html).

Ziniewicz, Gordon. "Experience, Education and Democracy." *Essays on the Philosophy of John Dewey*, 2000. Retrieved February 16, 2005 (http://www.fred.net/tzaka/preface.html).

INDEX

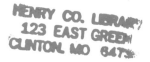

ABOUT THE AUTHOR

Amy Sterling Casil is a Southern California writer and college teacher. She is also the Director of Development for Beyond Shelter, an innovative nationally influential organization working with homeless families in the tradition of Jane Addams' Hull House.

PHOTO CREDITS

Cover (portrait), pp. 1, 12, 58, 72 © Getty Images; Cover (background), pp. 28, 48 © Bettmann/Corbis; p. 7 John Dewey Papers, Bentley Historical Library, University of Michigan; p. 9 © Corbis; pp. 17, 66, 83 © AP/WideWorld Photos; pp. 21, 26, 39, 45, 56, 73, 77 Library of Congress Prints and Photographs Division; p. 23 © Bridgeman Art Library; p. 31 The New York Public Library/Art Resource, NY; pp. 33, 64, 90–91 © Time-Life Pictures/Getty Images; pp. 34–35 Charles H. Cooley Papers, Bentley Historical Library, University of Michigan; p. 40 John Dewey, *The Ethics of Democracy*, (Ann Arbor, MI: University of Michigan. Philosophical papers, ser.2, no.1, 1888), Bentley Historical Library, University of Michigan; pp. 47, 80 The Granger Collection, New York; pp. 50, 55 Special Collections Research Center, Morris Library, Southern Illinois University, Carbondale; p. 68 © Arthur Rothstein/Corbis; p. 70 © Alfred A. Knopf; p. 75 Loyal University, New Orleans; p. 84 © Nubar Alexanian/Corbis; p. 88 Scala/Art Resource.

Designer: Gene Mollica; **Editor:** Nicholas Croce
Photo Researcher: Marty Levick